LGeW

# Around Us

**Ethics and Religious Culture
First Year of Elementary Cycle Two**

Élise Cardinal
Élisabeth Lacoste

## Student Book A

## Notice to Readers

There are many ways of writing certain terms specific to each religious tradition. The spelling used in this collection is the same as that used in the final version of the *Ethics and Religious Culture* elementary program.

LES ÉDITIONS
**CEC**
A Quebecor Media Company

9001, boul. Louis-H.-La Fontaine, Anjou (Québec) Canada  H1J 2C5
Telephone: 514 351-6010 • Fax: 514 351-3534

## ORIGINAL VERSION

**Publishing Manager**
Catherine Goyette

**Production Manager**
Danielle Latendresse

**Coordination Manager**
Rodolphe Courcy

**Project Manager and Linguistic Reviser**
Linda Tremblay

**Proofreader**
Jacinthe Caron

**Graphic Design, Graphic Production and Layout**

matteau parent
graphisme et communication
Geneviève Guérard and Chantale Richard-Nolin

## ENGLISH VERSION

**Translator**
Elizabeth Reeve

**Consultant**
Diana Popiel Kinach, Education Specialist, Riverside School Board

These programs are funded by Québec's Ministère de l'Éducation, du Loisir et du Sport, through contributions from the Canada-Québec Agreement on Minority-Language Education and Second-Language Instruction.

*Around Us*, Student Book A

© 2009, Les Éditions CEC inc.
9001, boul. Louis-H.-La Fontaine
Anjou, Québec H1J 2C5

Translation of *Autour de nous, Manuel A*
(ISBN 978-2-7617-2646-7)
© 2008, Les Éditions CEC inc.

Legal Deposit: 2009
Bibliothèque et Archives nationales du Québec
Library and Archives Canada

ISBN 978-2-7617-2873-7

Printed in Canada
2 3 4 5 13 12 11 10

**Illustrations**
Marie Lafrance (cover page), Julie Besançon (Module 1), Daniela Zekina (Modules 2 and 4), Volta Créations (Modules 3 and 8), Sophie Lewandowski (Modules 5 and 7), Benoît Laverdière (Module 6)

**Iconography Research**
Perrine Poiron and Jean-François Beaudette

The authors and the Publisher wish to thank the following people who took part in this project.

**Specialist Consultants (Ethics and Religious Culture)**
Pierre Després, Benoît Mercier, Benoît Patar, Robert Rousseau

**Educational Consultants**
Marlène Asselin, CS de la Seigneurie-des-Mille-Îles
Geneviève Bélanger, CS de la Pointe de l'Île
Josée Chrétien, CS de Montréal
Geneviève Prenoveau, CS de la Seigneurie-des-Mille-Îles
Mélanie Turcotte, CS des Grandes-Seigneuries

# Table of Contents

☐ : Religious Culture
☐ : Ethics

# Letter to the Student

Hi there!

In your *Around Us* Student Book, you will explore the world of Ethics and Religious Culture. Throughout, you will see pictures of pieces of fabric sewn together like in a quilt. There is a reason for this.

Think of the quilt as representing the society you live in. Like people, each piece is unique and different from the others, but is also part of a much larger whole. Each piece is joined to the others with thread. The thread can be compared to the relationships between people and the dialogue they use to communicate with one another. The better the quality of the thread, the more solid the quilt. Likewise, the more dialogue is respectful and effective, the easier it is to live together in harmony.

Come discover what is going on around you and your classmates.

Come discover this world, *Around Us …*

# Instructions

Each of the two **Around Us** Student Books has eight modules which develop competencies related to Ethics, Religious Culture and Dialogue. At the end of each book you will find a section called **The Dialogue Box**.

**Unik**, one of the mascots in the books, introduces the content. Unik appears in the books whenever there is an opportunity for dialogue. The other mascot, **Threddie**, is used in the features called **Threddie's Info**.

Unik

The module title introduces the theme covered.

Pieces of a quilt remind us that diversity helps create a harmonious whole. Also, each piece of fabric is paired with two modules.

Module 1

You, Me, Us

Do you think a human being can live alone? In this module, you will see that there are numerous advantages to living in a group. You will also discover that human beings help one another in many different ways.

A short text gives a preview of the content covered in the unit.

8

9

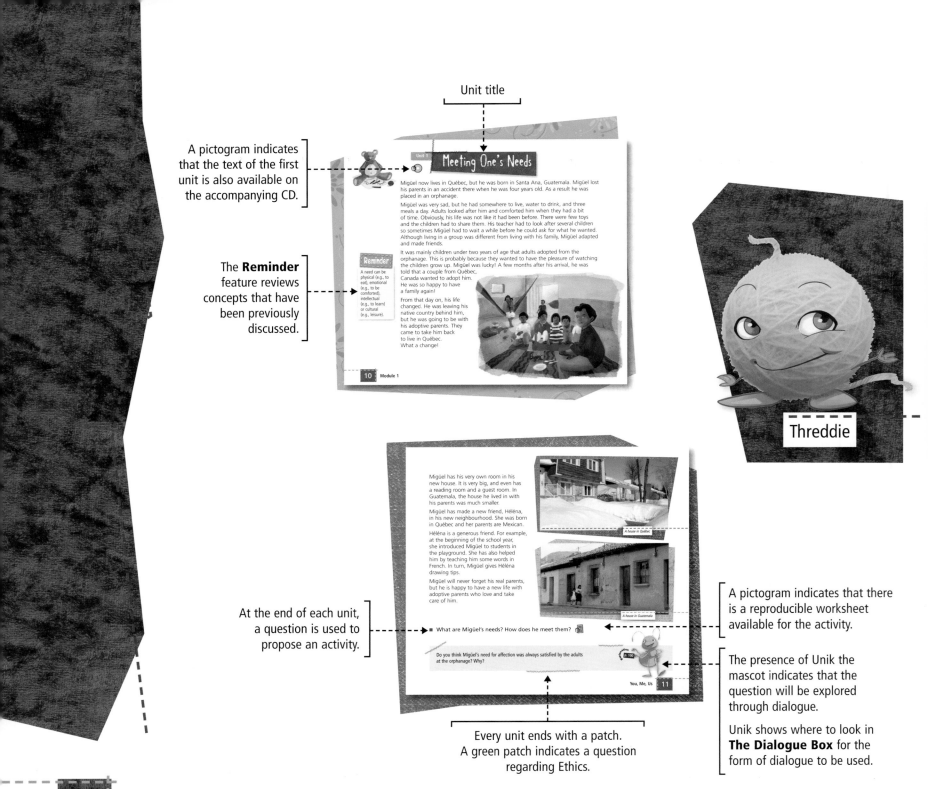

A pictogram indicates that the text of the first unit is also available on the accompanying CD.

The **Reminder** feature reviews concepts that have been previously discussed.

Threddie

At the end of each unit, a question is used to propose an activity.

A pictogram indicates that there is a reproducible worksheet available for the activity.

The presence of Unik the mascot indicates that the question will be explored through dialogue.

Unik shows where to look in **The Dialogue Box** for the form of dialogue to be used.

Every unit ends with a patch. A green patch indicates a question regarding Ethics.

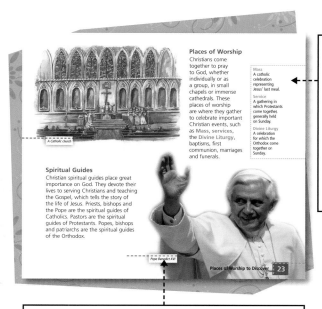

### Places of Worship

Christians come together to pray to God, whether individually or as a group, in small chapels or immense cathedrals. These places of worship are where they gather to celebrate important Christian events, such as Mass, services, the Divine Liturgy, baptisms, first communion, marriages and funerals.

**Mass**
A catholic celebration representing Jesus' last meal.

**Service**
A gathering in which Protestants come together, generally held on Sunday.

**Divine Liturgy**
A celebration for which the Orthodox come together on Sunday.

*A Catholic church*

### Spiritual Guides

Christian spiritual guides place great importance on God. They devote their lives to serving Christians and teaching the Gospel, which tells the story of the life of Jesus. Priests, bishops and the Pope are the spiritual guides of Catholics. Pastors are the spiritual guides of Protestants. Popes, bishops and patriarchs are the spiritual guides of the Orthodox.

*Pope Benedict XVI*

Places of Worship to Discover **23**

Words printed in blue in the text are defined in the margin to make the text easier to understand. These words are also listed in the glossary at the back of the Student Book.

**Threddie's Info** gives additional information about the topic, using a question-and-answer format.

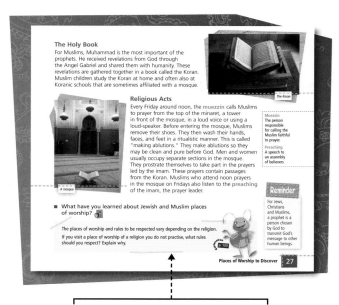

### The Holy Book

For Muslims, Muhammad is the most important of the prophets. He received revelations from God through the Angel Gabriel and shared them with humanity. These revelations are gathered together in a book called the Koran. Muslim children study the Koran at home and often also at Koranic schools that are sometimes affiliated with a mosque.

*The Koran*

### Religious Acts

Every Friday around noon, the muezzin calls Muslims to prayer from the top of the minaret, a tower in front of the mosque, in a loud voice or using a loud-speaker. Before entering the mosque, Muslims remove their shoes. They then wash their hands, faces, and feet in a ritualistic manner. This is called "making ablutions." They make ablutions so they may be clean and pure before God. Men and women usually occupy separate sections in the mosque. They prostrate themselves to take part in the prayers led by the imam. These prayers contain passages from the Koran. Muslims who attend noon prayers in the mosque on Fridays also listen to the preaching of the imam, the prayer leader.

*A mosque*

**Muezzin**
The person responsible for calling the Muslim faithful to prayer.

**Preaching**
A speech to an assembly of believers.

**Reminder**
For Jews, Christians and Muslims, a prophet is a person chosen by God to transmit God's message to other human beings.

■ What have you learned about Jewish and Muslim places of worship?

The places of worship and rules to be respected vary depending on the religion.

If you visit a place of worship of a religion you do not practise, what rules should you respect? Explain why.

Places of Worship to Discover **27**

A yellow patch indicates a question regarding Religious Culture.

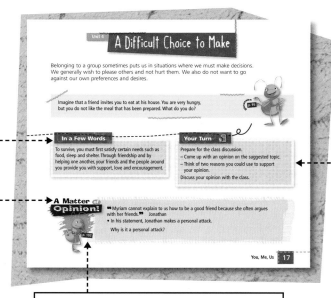

Unit 4
## A Difficult Choice to Make

Belonging to a group sometimes puts us in situations where we must make decisions. We generally wish to please others and not hurt them. We also do not want to go against our own preferences and desires.

Imagine that a friend invites you to eat at his house. You are very hungry, but you do not like the meal that has been prepared. What do you do?

### In a Few Words

To survive, you must first satisfy certain needs such as food, sleep and shelter. Through friendship and by helping one another, your friends and the people around you provide you with support, love and encouragement.

### Your Turn

Prepare for the class discussion.
– Come up with an opinion on the suggested topic.
– Think of two reasons you could use to support your opinion.
Discuss your opinion with the class.

### A Matter of Opinion!

"Myriam cannot explain to us how to be a good friend because she often argues with her friends." Jonathan
• In his statement, Jonathan makes a personal attack.
  Why is it a personal attack?

You, Me, Us **17**

The **In a Few Words** feature provides a summary of the module in preparation for the task in the **Your Turn** feature.

The **A Matter of Opinion!** feature at the end of each module proposes an activity involving the dialogue competency. These are oral exercises. They offer an opportunity to identify different means for examining a point of view (types of judgments and items that make dialogue more difficult).

The **Your Turn** feature presents a challenge. A reproducible worksheet has been provided to facilitate the challenge.

Unik, the mascot, shows where to look in **The Dialogue Box** for the form of dialogue to be used.

# You, Me, Us

Do you think a human being can live alone? In this module, you will see that there are numerous advantages to living in a group. You will also discover that human beings help one another in many different ways.

# Meeting One's Needs

Migüel now lives in Québec, but he was born in Santa Ana, Guatemala. Migüel lost his parents in an accident there when he was four years old. As a result he was placed in an orphanage.

Migüel was very sad, but he had somewhere to live, water to drink, and three meals a day. Adults looked after him and comforted him when they had a bit of time. Obviously, his life was not like it had been before. There were few toys and the children had to share them. His teacher had to look after several children so sometimes Migüel had to wait a while before he could ask for what he wanted. Although living in a group was different from living with his family, Migüel adapted and made friends.

It was mainly children under two years of age that adults adopted from the orphanage. This is probably because they wanted to have the pleasure of watching the children grow up. Migüel was lucky! A few months after his arrival, he was told that a couple from Québec, Canada wanted to adopt him. He was so happy to have a family again!

From that day on, his life changed. He was leaving his native country behind him, but he was going to be with his adoptive parents. They came to take him back to live in Québec. What a change!

## Reminder

A need can be physical (e.g., to eat), emotional (e.g., to be comforted), intellectual (e.g., to learn) or cultural (e.g., leisure).

Migüel has his very own room in his new house. It is very big, and even has a reading room and a guest room. In Guatemala, the house he lived in with his parents was much smaller.

Migüel has made a new friend, Héléna, in his new neighbourhood. She was born in Québec and her parents are Mexican.

Héléna is a generous friend. For example, at the beginning of the school year, she introduced Migüel to students in the playground. She has also helped him by teaching him some words in French. In turn, Migüel gives Héléna drawing tips.

Migüel will never forget his real parents, but he is happy to have a new life with adoptive parents who love and take care of him.

*A house in Québec*

*A house in Guatemala*

■ **What are Migüel's needs? How does he meet them?**

Do you think Migüel's need for affection was always satisfied by the adults at the orphanage? Why?

Explanation p. 100

# Helping One Another

You have surely been in situations where you needed others. Maybe someone then offered to help you. You in turn have undoubtedly lent a hand to someone you know. We say we are providing mutual assistance when we comfort or help one another.

## Community Service Organizations

**Volunteer**
A person who helps another freely and without being paid.

All over the world, **volunteers** help people in difficulty. Some volunteers join organizations to work together. Numerous community service organizations have been created over the years, each meeting different needs. For example, some supply clothing to people who are out of work, while others provide shelter for the homeless during periods of intense cold.

## Society of Saint Vincent de Paul

The Society of Saint Vincent de Paul is a well-known community service organization. It was founded by Frédéric Ozanam. Born in 1813, Frédéric was brought up in Lyon, France, by his parents, who helped poor people. When he was twenty he founded the Society of Saint Vincent de Paul in honour of Vincent de Paul, a Catholic priest who devoted his life to helping others.

Frédéric had one wish: to help people in need. His dream has become a reality, as the Society of Saint Vincent de Paul now has thousands of volunteer members around the world helping people living in poverty, regardless of their nationality or religion. Here are two activities run by this organization.

**Reminder**

The Christian family includes Catholic, Protestant and Orthodox churches.

The Grande Guignolée is an annual holiday food drive by media organizations. Hundreds of volunteers, in various parts of Québec, appeal to the generosity of the public, collecting money and foodstuffs. The food drive helps the Society of Saint Vincent de Paul and other organizations feed families living in poverty during the holiday season.

Operation Bonne Mine has existed since 1994. It raises money for children in disadvantaged neighbourhoods to buy necessary school supplies at the beginning of the school year and take part in cultural outings and extracurricular activities.

Recreational activities are organized for people with disabilities. They make it easier for the disabled to integrate into society and help them have confidence in themselves.

Respect for others and helping one another are values young people put into practice at the day camp.

## The YMCA

The Englishman George Williams founded the first YMCA (*Young Men's Christian Association*), another community service organization inspired by Protestant evangelicalism. In his youth, George Williams had to work long days under very difficult conditions. He would meet with other young Christian workers like himself at a community centre, to talk, meditate and pray. Together, they decided to join forces to help people living in poverty.

The first YMCA in Canada was founded in Montréal in 1851. The mission and the activities of the organization have evolved so as to serve and help people of all ages and origins.

Here are two examples of activities organized by the Montréal YMCA.

■ **What would you do if you decided to help the people in the situations shown on page 12?**

The YMHA (*Young Men's Hebrew Association*), run by people of the Jewish faith, is an organization that performs community services. Volunteers raise money to help children living in poverty or with physical or mental disabilities take part in various activities.

Do you know another community service organization? Describe it.

Description  p. 99

# Acts of Friendship

Living with others makes it easier to develop supportive, friendly relationships. People meet, speak and get to know one another. They discover common interests and tastes. We often create friendships through recreational activities.

Have you ever heard of the Scouts? Throughout the world, millions of young people of all origins are part of the Scout Movement. It was started over 100 years ago by Robert Baden-Powell, son of an Anglican pastor and a general in the British army. Friendship, helping one another and respect for God were very important values to him. He brought young people together to teach them to do their best and to do a good deed every day.

Here are some scouts who have become friends.

❝I met my best friend Maya in Beaver Scouts. We both like to sing and play scouting games.❞
Julia

❝In Cub Scouts, I discovered that Julien was as interested in nature as I was. We both like to build the fire when we go camping.❞     Samuel

❝I got to know Alexia better at summer camp. When we did rock painting, I saw she was as painstaking about it as I was, because she paid attention to small details.❞     Annabelle

Friends understand and respect one another; they listen to and help each other. Here are some things children your age have done to strengthen their friendships.

“My friend Elliot uses a wheelchair to get around. I like playing basketball with him, even if he is different.”    Youri

“When my best friend Julia gets a perfect mark on her math exam, I congratulate her even if I am very envious.”

Charlie

“The grandmother of my friend Sofia just died. Sofia is not coming to the pool with me. I understand she wants to be alone to grieve.”

Maéva

“My friend Marissa is adopted. She did not have enough to eat before she began living with her adoptive family. I understand why she sometimes hides food.”

Émile

“There's no pleasure like meeting an old friend, except, perhaps, making a new one.”

Rudyard Kipling, *The Enlightenments of Pagett, M.P.*, Volume IV Under The Deodars, By Macmillan and Co., 1895.

■ **You have seen what friendship means to Rudyard Kipling. In your opinion, what qualities make a person a good friend?**

Friendships develop for different reasons. Sometimes, we become friends because we are alike. Other times, we become friends because, though different, we complement one another.

Do you believe it is easier to become friends with someone who is like you or someone who complements you? Why?

Comparison
p. 99

# A Difficult Choice to Make

Belonging to a group sometimes puts us in situations where we must make decisions. We generally wish to please others and not hurt them. We also do not want to go against our own preferences and desires.

Imagine that a friend invites you to eat at his house. You are very hungry, but you do not like the meal that has been prepared. What do you do?

*Discussion* p. 95

## In a Few Words

To survive, you must first satisfy certain needs such as food, sleep and shelter. Through friendship and by helping one another, your friends and the people around you provide you with support, love and encouragement.

## Your Turn

Prepare for the class discussion.

– Come up with an opinion on the suggested topic.

– Think of two reasons you could use to support your opinion.

Discuss your opinion with the class.

## A Matter of Opinion!

p. 102

66 Myriam cannot explain to us how to be a good friend because she often argues with her friends. 99   Jonathan

• In his statement, Jonathan makes a personal attack.

Why is it a personal attack?

# Places of Worship to Discover

Are there certain places where you are used to getting together with friends, family or the people you love? People who practise the same religion usually come together in a place they consider sacred, their place of worship. In this module, you will discover different places of worship and spiritual guides.

# Charlie's Photos

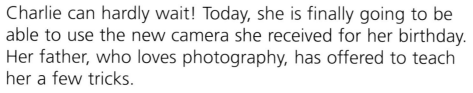

Charlie can hardly wait! Today, she is finally going to be able to use the new camera she received for her birthday. Her father, who loves photography, has offered to teach her a few tricks.

Outside, the sun is shining, illuminating the autumn leaves. It is a perfect day to learn about photography. Charlie is proud to be going on an outing in the city alone with her father. She skips along happily on the sidewalk, camera in hand. She hears a carillon in the distance. Curious, Charlie walks faster.

She comes to a large stone building. With its two great towers, it makes her think of a castle. She admires the statues, the stained-glass windows and the three arches at the entrance. There is also a large cross on the doors. Her father explains to her that it is a cathedral, a big church where certain Christians go to pray. Charlie finally takes her first photos.

"Dad, do people who practise other religions also get together in special places?"

"Yes, those people come together in their own places of worship to practise their religion. When we get home, I will show you some of these places I photographed in the countries I have visited."

At home, Charlie turns the pages of the photo albums of her father's travels. A bronze statue catches her eye.

"Dad, my friend Katsouko has the same statue in her house!"

"It is a statue of Buddha. Look behind it. You can see a pagoda, where Buddhists go to worship."

In another photo, Charlie notices women wearing brightly coloured clothing. Her father explains that the building on their left is a Hindu temple and that those women go there periodically to make offerings to the deities.

Charlie's father shows her a photograph of another place. He explains that it is a synagogue, a place of worship where Jews come together. Above the double doors is a beautiful stained-glass window with a white and blue star.

Charlie asks if all these places of worship exist in her city because she would like to take photographs of them. Her father explains to her that many of them do, but not all have the same architecture as in the photographs. Charlie cannot wait to photograph the places of worship in her city.

■ **What is the name of the place of worship for Jewish people? for Buddhists? for Hindus? for Christians?**

Stained-glass windows were used to represent Bible stories. This was especially useful for people who did not know how to read. Nowadays, stained-glass windows are found all over and are no longer used only to depict religious scenes.

Have you ever seen a stained-glass window? Describe what it represents.

Description   p. 99

# Christian Places of Worship

**Place of worship**
A place where believers gather together to pay homage to a deity.

Catholics, Protestants and the Orthodox are part of the big Christian family. They all believe in God, but they separated long ago because they did not completely agree on certain questions. Orthodoxy began in the 13th century while Protestantism began in the 16th century. Their **places of worship** and spiritual guides are not all the same.

*Our Lady of Kazan Church, Rawdon*

*Saint Joseph's Oratory in Montréal*

*Sainte-Marcelline Church, Sainte-Marcelline-de-Kildare*

*A Catholic church*

## Places of Worship

Christians come together to pray to God, whether individually or as a group, in small chapels or immense cathedrals. These places of worship are where they gather to celebrate important Christian events, such as **Mass**, **services**, the **Divine Liturgy**, baptisms, first communion, marriages and funerals.

**Mass**
A catholic celebration representing Jesus' last meal.

**Service**
A gathering in which Protestants come together, generally held on Sunday.

**Divine Liturgy**
A celebration for which the Orthodox come together on Sunday.

## Spiritual Guides

Christian spiritual guides place great importance on God. They devote their lives to serving Christians and teaching the Gospel, which tells the story of the life of Jesus. Priests, bishops and the Pope are the spiritual guides of Catholics. Pastors are the spiritual guides of Protestants. Popes, bishops and patriarchs are the spiritual guides of the Orthodox.

*Pope Benedict XVI*

## The Holy Book

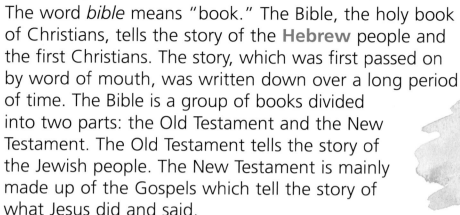

The word *bible* means "book." The Bible, the holy book of Christians, tells the story of the **Hebrew** people and the first Christians. The story, which was first passed on by word of mouth, was written down over a long period of time. The Bible is a group of books divided into two parts: the Old Testament and the New Testament. The Old Testament tells the story of the Jewish people. The New Testament is mainly made up of the Gospels which tell the story of what Jesus did and said.

**Hebrew**
That which relates to the Hebrews, the ancestors of the Jewish people.

**Sermon**
A speech by a pastor or lay preacher and based on one or more biblical texts.

## Religious Acts

Christians usually gather in church on Sundays to listen to the Word of God, to pray and to sing. For Catholics, this gathering is called the "Mass." Protestants call it a "service" and the Orthodox call it the "Divine Liturgy." Catholics sit or kneel in front of the altar while texts from the Bible are being read. The priest comments on these texts. By repeating the same gestures Jesus performed at his last meal, the priest helps Catholics remember the death and resurrection of Jesus. Then, Catholics take Communion, meaning they receive the Host. In Protestant services, the pastor reads passages from the Bible and then delivers a **sermon** to explain their meaning. Protestants do not take Communion every Sunday.

■ **What have you learned about the places of worship of Catholics? Protestants? Orthodox?**

Maybe you have seen or visited a church before.

If so, what caught your attention? Discuss the topic with your classmates.

Conversation
p. 95

# Other Places of Worship

## A Visit to a Synagogue

Jews practise one of the oldest religions in the world. They come together in the synagogue to pray to God, to celebrate, and to study the Torah, their holy book.

### The Holy Book

The Jewish people study the Torah. It is the first five books of the Tanakh, the Hebrew Bible. The Jews believe that God gave them these texts to guide them in their daily lives. The Torah is presented in the form of scrolls. In the synagogue, it is placed in a special cupboard called the Ark.

Jews also study the Talmud, a book that contains scholarly commentary on the Torah, among other things.

## Threddie's Info

**Why do Jews cover their heads in the synagogue?**

It is a sign of respect towards God for them. Many men wear the kippa, a small cap, on top of the head during prayer, while others wear it all the time. Some married women cover their hair with scarves, hats, berets or wigs either during prayer or all the time.

### Religious Acts

The day of Sabbath lasts from sunset on Friday until sunset on Saturday. Practising Jews go to a synagogue to pray and to listen to a passage from the Torah. The rabbi mounts the bimah, a platform in the middle of the synagogue, and explains the passage being presented. Men wear a tallit, or prayer shawl, to pray. They also wear **tefillins**, with one on the left arm and one on the forehead.

*A synagogue*

**Tefillin**
A pair of boxes containing excerpts from the Torah, which certain practising Jewish men wear on the forehead and left arm during prayer.

## Visit to a Mosque

Muslims like to come together in the main hall of the mosque on Fridays to pray to God.

## The Holy Book

For Muslims, Muhammad is the most important of the prophets. He received revelations from God through the Angel Gabriel and shared them with humanity. These revelations are gathered together in a book called the Koran. Muslim children study the Koran at home and often also at Koranic schools that are sometimes affiliated with a mosque.

*The Koran*

## Religious Acts

*A mosque*

Every Friday around noon, the **muezzin** calls Muslims to prayer from the top of the minaret, a tower in front of the mosque, in a loud voice or using a loud-speaker. Before entering the mosque, Muslims remove their shoes. They then wash their hands, faces, and feet in a ritualistic manner. This is called "making ablutions." They make ablutions so they may be clean and pure before God. Men and women usually occupy separate sections in the mosque. They prostrate themselves to take part in the prayers led by the imam. These prayers contain passages from the Koran. Muslims who attend noon prayers in the mosque on Fridays also listen to the **preaching** of the imam, the prayer leader.

**Muezzin**
The person responsible for calling the Muslim faithful to prayer.

**Preaching**
A speech to an assembly of believers

**Reminder**

For Jews, Christians and Muslims, a prophet is a person chosen by God to transmit God's message to other human beings.

■ **What have you learned about Jewish and Muslim places of worship?**

The places of worship and rules to be respected vary depending on the religion.

If you visit a place of worship of a religion you do not practise, what rules should you respect? Explain why.

Explanation p. 100

# Other Forms of Worship

*Meenakshi temple in Madurai, India*

As well as coming together in their places of worship, Hindus and Buddhists have a place in their home where they pray as a family.

## Guided Tour

### In the Hindu Home

Hindus have numerous gods. The best known are Vishnu, Shiva, Krishna and Rama. Hindus sometimes go to pray and make offerings in temples. A guru, the Hindus' spiritual guide, presents these offerings to the gods, while chanting. Every day, Hindus perform Puja at home: seated before the image of one of their gods, they recite prayers while burning incense. They also make offerings of water, flowers and grains of rice.

### In the Buddhist Home

Buddhists do not have a god. They follow the teachings of Buddha, which promote the virtues of a life of peace. Buddhists go to the pagoda to make offerings of food and flowers. Monks in monasteries teach them the life and ideas of Buddha. Like Hindus, Buddhists perform Puja at home every day. They recite prayers while burning incense before a small altar that has a picture or statue of Buddha.

*A Buddhist pagoda in China*

The architecture of the places of worship found in Québec varies depending on the religion. The oldest are Native, Catholic, Protestant or Jewish. These places are all part of the religious heritage of Québec.

## In a Few Words

Churches, synagogues, mosques, temples and pagodas are places where believers come together to practise their beliefs. In most of these places of worship, spiritual guides lead religious celebrations. They tell people about the words and writings that inspire their religious community and offer guidance to believers.

## Your Turn

Make a poster of one of these places of worship for an exhibit.

On your poster, describe and illustrate the building, the spiritual guide and a religious act related to the place of worship.

## A Matter of Opinion!

p. 101

66 My teacher taught me that over 800 years ago the King of France and the Bishop of Paris decided to build Paris' Notre-Dame Cathedral. Construction of the cathedral began in 1163 and took over 100 years to complete. 99    Dominique

- In giving this information on the Paris cathedral, Dominique makes a judgment of reality. Check whether what she says is true or false.
  - Where does Dominique's information come from?
  - Is his source reliable?

# On the Way to Harmony

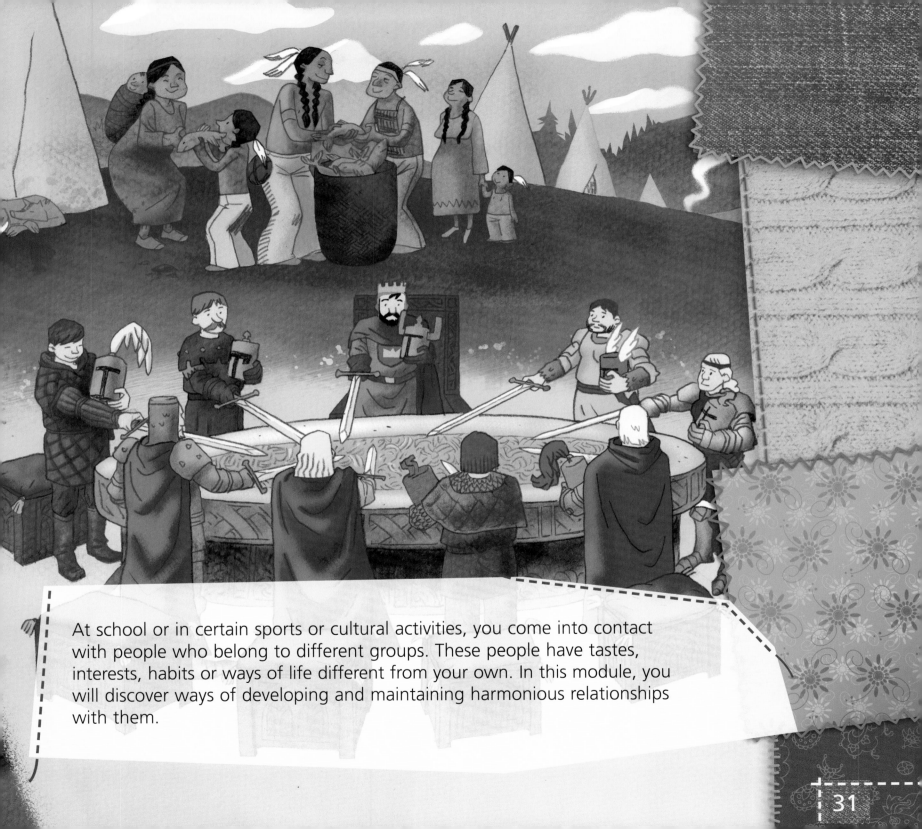

At school or in certain sports or cultural activities, you come into contact with people who belong to different groups. These people have tastes, interests, habits or ways of life different from your own. In this module, you will discover ways of developing and maintaining harmonious relationships with them.

# Speaking Up

Anonkwe is a shy boy. He sometimes has difficulty saying what he thinks. He is hesitant to give his opinion in groups. At the class meeting today, he wanted to talk about a problem he has been experiencing in the schoolyard, but his shyness kept him from speaking up.

To take his mind off his problems when he gets home, he suggests to his big sister Arakwa that they go for a walk in the park. There are enormous trees, paths, and small animals in the park. Arakwa is a nature-lover and takes the time to explain what she knows to her brother. Today, Anonkwe and Arakwa watch birds through their binoculars.

"I love birds. They are so colourful! And they look like they live together peacefully," says Anonkwe.

"Birds do often live in harmony with one another. However, when you have observed them more, you will see that they sometimes have disagreements," answers Arakwa. "I find that when human beings are in groups, they often behave like birds."

"Really?"

"Yes. In fact, each bird species behaves differently depending on the situation. You and I do that too. We do not act the same way with our family as we do in class. In fact, look at the black bird on the branch. It is a European starling. It imitates the songs of other bird species."

"Starlings should find their own song," says Anonkwe.

"I absolutely agree with you. When we do not really know what we think, when we say the same thing as others without giving our real opinion, we behave a bit like starlings! Hey, look on that branch over there. That is a brown-headed cowbird."

"What is special about that type of bird?"

"Cowbirds do not build nests. The females lay their eggs in the nests of other species and leave their young there. They take places that do not belong to them."

"I think there are people like that in life too, who do not leave enough room for others. Do you know any?" asks Anonkwe.

"Yes! I behaved that way with you in the past. When you were little, I answered in your place when people asked you questions. It made you so angry! Here, take the binoculars. Look at the top of the fir tree. That is an Eastern bluebird."

"I have never seen one before," says Anonkwe.

*A European starling*

*A brown-headed cowbird*

*An Eastern bluebird*

"Probably because the number of bluebirds has gone down a lot. There are fewer and fewer of them, because birds like starlings are moving into the areas where bluebirds like to build their nests. One could say that bluebirds do not stand up for themselves enough."

"What is that little yellow and black bird?" asks Anonkwe.

"That is a goldfinch. Goldfinch are sociable and like being in the company of other birds. They have a unique song of their own. They take their place while tolerating others."

"I have an idea. We will try to see what type of bird we most resemble," says Anonkwe.

"Good idea!"

*A Goldfinch*

■ **What type of bird do you resemble when you are at school? with your group of friends?**

Anonkwe has difficulty speaking up in class.

What advice would you give him?

Conversation
p. 95

# Harmonious Interpersonal Relationships

A harmonious interpersonal relationship is a relationship in which people **reciprocally** show respect. In a harmonious relationship, people listen to one another, understand one another and support one another. They also take differences between them into consideration in order to be fair.

**Reciprocally**
In the same way to each other

**Empathy**
Ability to put oneself in the place of another, to understand what the other person feels.

## Among Friends

When we express our ideas, feelings and opinions, and when we listen to others and show **empathy**, we are on the path to a harmonious relationship.

66 I listen to my friends when they speak to me. I ask them questions, because I am interested in what they tell me. When it is my turn and I have something to say, my friends do the same thing. 99      Alexis

66 When my friend is sad, I comfort her. I try to put myself in her shoes to understand her better. When I am the one with a problem, my friend helps me find solutions. 99      Anaïs

## In Families

When we are fair to one another and we take our differences into account, we are also on the way to building a harmonious relationship. Children want adults to treat them fairly at school and at home. That is why most parents take their children's ages into account when granting them privileges and establishing their responsibilities.

"My little brother is three years old. My parents do not allow him to go to bed at the same time as I do! We have different privileges. We also have different responsibilities. I have to make my bed every morning, but my brother is still too little. Because I am older, I have more responsibilities. I think that is fair." Patrick

## In Other Groups

When we support one another, we are also on the way to harmony. In the past, most Native nations had a chief. Chiefs did not give orders to the members of their village, but made sure they had the community's consent before making a decision. In that way, they respected the desires of the people in their communities and did not impose anything on them. Chiefs defended the group's opinion: they supported the people of their village.

Do you know the legend of the Knights of the Round Table? The story is approximately one thousand years old, and tells of King Arthur and his courageous companions, who were responsible for ensuring the peace of the kingdom. They worked together for the same cause. When the knights gathered together around the famous table, its round shape reminded them that they were all equal, like brothers.

■ **Which situations reflect harmonious relationships?**

Harmonious relationships contribute to developing friendliness and respect. What might harmonious relationships look like at school? With your friends?

p. 99

Description

# Cooperation in the Classroom

Cooperation encourages harmony in groups and helps us get along together better. Cooperation is working together with the same goal, to accomplish a common task.

In schools most classes hold class meetings or class cooperation meetings, somewhat like the Knights of the Round Table.

The students in the class come together with the teacher for a discussion. They sit in a circle and talk about what is going well in the class and what is not going as well: responsibilities, games, projects, interpersonal relationships, etc. This is a time when harmonious relationships are especially encouraged. Each child has an equal voice and the right to be treated with respect. Differences of opinion are accepted. When there is a decision to be made, the class generally tries to do so by reaching a **consensus**.

**Consensus**
A common decision, agreement reached in a group.

66 All students take part in decision-making. There is no leader, and nobody receives special preference. We try to find solutions that suit the entire group. When we are unable to, our teacher makes the final decision. 99    Emmanuel

Cooperation is appropriate for a class meeting. There are other occasions when we can cooperate. We can join forces and help each other to complete a task. Here are some examples.

Creating a work of art, like a mural.

Organizing a special event, like a party.

Planning a class outing, like a visit to a museum.

Do you know the story of the *Three Musketeers*? It was written by Alexandre Dumas in 1844. It tells of four soldiers, the musketeers, who were given the mission of protecting the King and Queen of France. Although they were different, they knew how to pool their strengths and talents. Their rallying cry, expressing solidarity and cooperation, may be familiar to you: *All for one, one for all!*

■ Imagine what might have happened to the characters of some well-known stories if they had cooperated with one another (The Grasshopper and the Ant, Hansel and Gretel, etc.)?

In sports competitions, athletes measure themselves against one another.

In your opinion, what are the similarities and differences between competition and cooperation?

Comparison p. 99

# A Tale of Harmony

This is the story of a day in the life of Sondokwa, a young Algonquin. It takes place over five hundred years ago. Even then, Sondokwa and the other members of his camp already knew how to maintain harmonious relationships.

It is a good day for fishing. Sondokwa stands beside his father, harpoon in hand. Sondokwa hopes to catch a lot of fish. That way, when he gets back to camp, he will be able to share his catch. The fishermen work together to make sure all the camp's inhabitants will be able to eat their fill.

Sondokwa likes to learn from his father, who is very patient. His father explains the right way to do things and treats him as an equal.

Tonight, Sondokwa's father will be taking part in a meeting of the clan council because he is the chief. He may get home very late at night, as he must discuss certain points with the other members of the council until everybody agrees.

## In a Few Words

There are several ways to keep harmonious and egalitarian relationships in a group. Showing respect, listening to others, and cooperating are some examples.

## Your Turn

Imagine you are helping Unik prepare a meeting of his book club. What advice would you give Unik so the meeting runs harmoniously?

– List three pieces of advice you would give Unik.

– Use examples to explain them.

**A Matter of Opinion!**

p. 102

❝Mom, I want to go to bed late tonight. My friends say that once you turn nine, you can go to sleep whenever you want.❞     Jean-Sébastien

• Do you think Jean-Sébastien's argument is convincing?

Explain your answer.

# Responsible Children

Children have rights, but they also have responsibilities.

In this module, you will learn that, depending on the place where they live, children have roles and responsibilities that are sometimes very different from yours in Québec.

# Mélissandre's Voyage

This morning, Mélissandre does not have to do chores. She is lazing around in her berth, while her brother and sister are busy on deck. Although rays of sun pierce through the clouds, they are not strong enough to chase away the morning humidity on the Peruvian coast. For some months now, Mélissandre and her family have been living on *The Explorer,* the family sailboat. Mélissandre, Malek and Mia were introduced to the joys of sailing by their parents, Thierry and Luccia, at a very early age.

At a family meeting last year, they decided to travel to Peru, home of their maternal ancestors. Living on a boat as a family is a wonderful experience, but a few minor adjustments were necessary in the beginning. The children did not always feel like doing their math exercises or writing in their logbooks. Although swimming with the fishes and daydreaming in a hammock are very pleasant, there are many chores to do on a boat and everyone has to do their share. It was therefore necessary to set out everybody's roles and responsibilities.

"Imagine our sailboat is like a big stage where each person has a role to play. As we are your parents, it is our responsibility to take care of you, educate you and protect you," says Luccia.

"As I am the most experienced navigator, I also play the role of captain," says Thierry.

"Oh, I understand, Dad! As Malek, Mia and I are children, it will be our responsibility to help you."

"Yes, Mélissandre! That is why you will each have your own chores," said the father, ruffling his eldest daughter's hair.

"Now it is time to play your student's role! As well as the mom's role, I also play the role of teacher. Captain Thierry, make sure you set the anchor properly."

In the morning, Mélissandre, her brother and sister devote themselves to schoolwork. In the afternoon, they do the chores they are responsible for. Today, Malek and Mia are the apprentice cooks. They will gut and scale the fish. Mélissandre is doing the shopping. She likes this role. It is her turn to go with her mother to the local market to buy potatoes. She hopes she will see Tomasino, a young Quechua Indian she met on her last trip to the market. She has prepared a small surprise for him: sheets of paper and pencils he will be able to use to write to her.

Tomasino lives in the mountains. Where he lives, everybody helps to do the work in the fields. As his family is poor and the high school is in the city, far from his home, Tomasino no longer goes to school. This way, he can help his family. He misses going to school, but he is proud to be doing his part and does not complain. Tomasino does not have running water or electricity in his home. His sisters and he are responsible for getting water from the well and gathering wood to heat the house.

Tomasino considers himself lucky that he and his grandparents, parents and six sisters are still living in their house. Its walls are built of earth and straw, and it was not destroyed in the last earthquake.

Mélissandre is happy to see Tomasino again. She realizes that their lives are not at all alike. Tomasino seems happy despite all his responsibilities.

■ **What are the roles and responsibilities of the members of Mélissandre's family? of Tomasino?**
   **What roles and responsibilities do you have?**

In Québec, children are obliged by law to attend school until the age of sixteen.

In your opinion, why is it necessary to go to school?

p. 100
Explanation

# Roles and Responsibilities

In life, people are called on to play different roles. In your family, you may be the protective big brother or the entertaining big sister. With your group of friends, you may be the person in whom the others confide, or whom others ask for help. You may be the captain on your soccer team. Your responsibilities vary according to your role.

As responsibilities also depend on a person's age, adults have more responsibilities than children. For example, parents are responsible for taking care of their children's needs. They also pass their values and beliefs on to them. That is why in some families children make their own lunches, while in others they are obliged to make their beds.

Every child, girl or boy, rich or poor, has the right to be cared for, to go to school and to be safe, regardless of colour, religion or background. All children also have the right to express their opinions. That is what the United Nations Convention on the Rights of the Child says. This official document is a promise and agreement made in 1989 by almost all countries to guarantee the well-being of the children of the world.

However, there are countries where these rights are not respected. For example, some families are so poor that the only way they can survive is to have their children work.

# Kiran, a Child at Work

Kiran is nine years old. He lives in Calcutta, India. Before heavy rains destroyed the harvest, he lived in the countryside. He helped his family cultivate the field of wheat and went to school. Now that his family lives in the city, his father works fifteen hours a day in a factory, his mother shines shoes and his brother pulls people in a small ricksha. Kiran no longer goes to school because his parents do not have money for school supplies. He also must work to help feed his family. He sometimes sells objects he finds in the dump. Other times, he begs for money.

He regularly goes to the temple with his parents to pray and make offerings to Ganesha, the god with an elephant's head, so Ganesha will bring him luck. He continues to pray and hopes that one day he will be able to go back to school.

■ **Which of Kiran's rights have not been respected? Why?**

There are children who must work to survive.

In your opinion, is that too big a responsibility for these children? Why?

Explanation
p. 100

# Important People

Some people play an important role in your life. They teach you things, listen to you and guide you simply by being with you and by the things they do. They want to help you become more and more responsible.

## A Special Babysitter

**"** I always look forward to having Émilie baby-sit me. She has good arts and crafts ideas. She teaches me new drawing techniques and games of strategy. Since she showed me how to play chess, it has become a passion of mine! I was put in charge of the chess club at school.**"**    Rosalie

## An Inspiring Priest

**"** Last year, my family and I took part in a clothing drive for children in Bangladesh. I donated all the clothes that were too small for me. Roger, the priest at my church, told me about the lives of children in poor countries. Since then, helping people in need has been important to me. At the next class meeting, I am going to suggest we hold a stuffed animal drive for sick children in our area.**"**    Joël

In Japan, for example, academic success is extremely important. Schoolchildren have "masters." Their role is important, because they are responsible for helping their students strive for personal excellence.

## Aoki's Masters

Aoki is nine years old. She lives in the heart of Tokyo, a Japanese city full of neon lights and giant screens. She arrives at school, at 6:30 in the morning and greets her master Sho by bowing to him in a sign of respect. At school, she must obey her master as he represents knowledge and wisdom. For Aoki, like for most Japanese, it is very important to do well. Sho is an excellent teacher. He explains to her the things she does not understand and helps her improve. He teaches her the Japanese alphabet, Japanese calligraphy, mathematics, science, drawing, music, martial arts and origami.

**Lotus position**
Meditation position with the right foot on the left thigh, the left foot on the right thigh and the body as straight as possible.

Aoki is always very busy. Every day after school and during the summer holidays, she takes extra classes to improve her grades at school. Two evenings a week, she goes to the temple to practise meditation, which helps her concentrate better. Yuki, her Buddhist master, teaches her breathing techniques and how to sit in the **lotus position**.

Aoki is happy, because her parents and masters are proud of her. Her dearest wish is to go to one of the best universities in Japan, one day.

■ **What are the roles and responsibilities of children in Japan?**

For Aoki, her parents and masters are important people because they guide her.

Who helps you become more responsible? How?

Description
p. 99

# Differences

Québec is part of a country where children's rights must be respected. Unfortunately, in Québec, like elsewhere, those rights are not always respected.

Do you think the roles and responsibilities of children in Québec are the same as or different from those of Tomasino, Kiran and Aoki?

Comparison
p. 99

## In a Few Words

According to the Convention on the Rights of the Child, all children should have the same rights. Children also have responsibilities and obligations. These responsibilities may differ depending on where they live and on family values and beliefs.

## Your Turn

Prepare to answer Unik's question.

– Form an opinion on the suggested topic.

– Think of two reasons you could use to support your opinion.

Discuss your opinion with the class.

## A Matter of Opinion!

p. 101

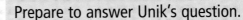

**"I prefer helping my parents cook to walking the dog."** Éva

• In her statement, Éva makes a judgment of preference.

What questions could you ask Éva to learn the reasons for her preference?

Can Éva always do what she prefers first?

# The Blue Planet

Chile's Lake Chungara, with the
reflection of Parinacota Volcano

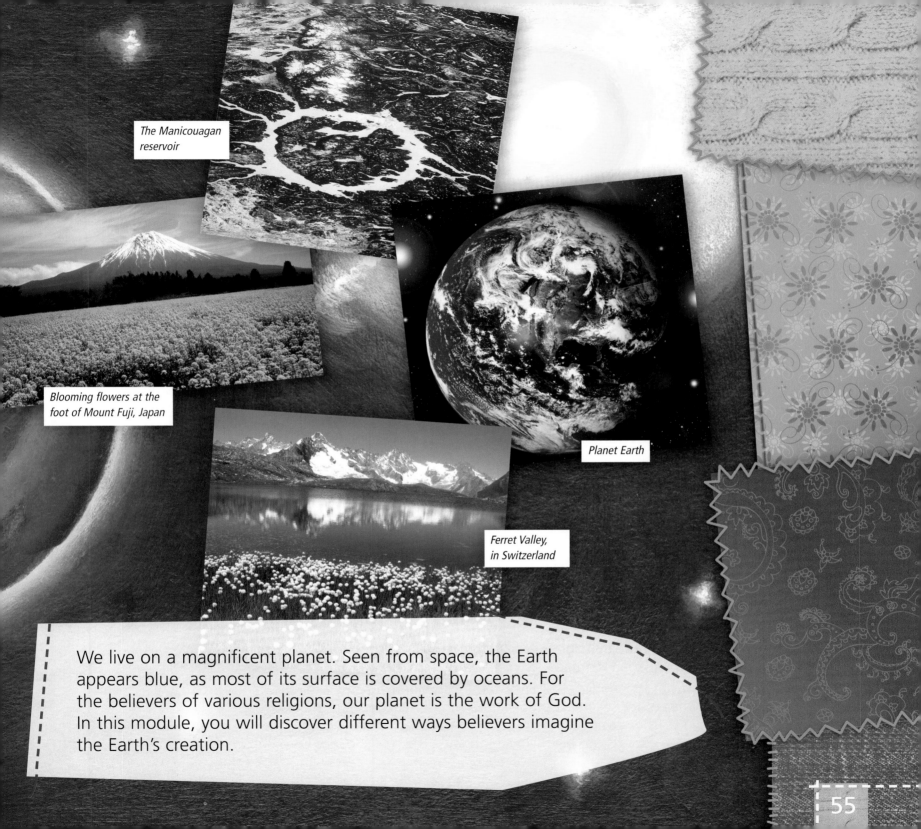

The Manicouagan reservoir

Blooming flowers at the foot of Mount Fuji, Japan

Planet Earth

Ferret Valley, in Switzerland

We live on a magnificent planet. Seen from space, the Earth appears blue, as most of its surface is covered by oceans. For the believers of various religions, our planet is the work of God. In this module, you will discover different ways believers imagine the Earth's creation.

# Words and Expressions

There is no school today. A storm is raging outdoors, so Laurent is playing in his bedroom. He is glad to have some time to have fun.

His mother knocks on the door and comes in. She says to him:

"Laurent, I would like you to tidy your bedroom a little. Could you put away your toys, hang your clean clothes in the closet and make your bed?"

When she sees her son's downcast expression, Laurent's mother exclaims:

"Is cleaning your room that hard? If you need help, I will give you a hand."

"No, Mom, I will manage. Thank you," replies Laurent.

Laurent sets to work. He finishes cleaning his room one hour later. He is very pleased, and asks his mother to come see the result. When she comes in, she exclaims:

"My God! It is so clean in here."

Laurent answers:

"Yes, I put everything away and I even dusted. But Mom, why are you talking to God?"

## Threddie's Info

**Why does our language today contain expressions related to the Christian religion?**

The Christian religion has been the most widely practised religion in Québec for several centuries. In the past, Quebecers were very devout. They used many expressions related to religion. Some of these expressions are still used today.

"To God? Oh, I understand. I used the expression 'My God' to express the surprise I felt at seeing your room so tidy. But I was not talking to God nor was I talking about religion. Sometimes we say 'My God' in everyday language when we are astonished, surprised or astounded. It is an expression that comes from the Christian religion."

"Mom, do the believers of other religions use the same name for God?"

"No, when speaking to God, Christians say 'God' or 'Lord.' Muslims use the Arabic word 'Allah,' which simply means 'God,' while Jews sometimes use 'Adonai,' which means 'my Lord.'

Did you know that in most religions, people believe that God created the universe and that God existed before all other things? But there are many different stories of the world's creation. Would you like me to tell them to you?"

"Good idea!" says Laurent.

- ■ **Do you know the meaning of other expressions related to specific religions?**

From among the expressions presented, which do you hear most often? Discuss this with your classmates.

# The Wonders of Nature

Protecting the planet became a real concern when people understood that the lives of living beings were dependent on it.

For people who believe in God, protecting the environment is also a mark of respect for what God has created. According to their beliefs, God is the creator of the universe, our planet and all the living beings on it. Several stories of the Creation are told in the Hebrew Bible (also called the Old Testament by Christians). This story also appears in the Koran, the sacred book of Muslims.

## Threddie's Info

**Do Christians, Jews and Muslims reject scientific explanations of the Earth's origin?**

The vast majority of Christians, Jews and Muslims accept scientific explanations of the origin of the world. For them, scientific theories explain how the planet Earth was formed, while Creation stories are texts that show how God is the master of the Earth and the Universe. On the other hand, there are some believers who reject scientific explanations of how the Earth was formed. Instead, they opt for a literal reading of the Bible, which tells how the Earth was created in six days.

## The Story of Creation

In the beginning, God created the heaven and the Earth.
There was nothing on Earth. There was darkness everywhere.
The spirit of God hovered over the waters.
God said: *Let there be light!* And there was light.
God called the light "Day" and the darkness "Night."
There was the first morning.
It was the first day.

God said: *Let there be a heaven above the waters*.
There was an evening and there was a morning.
It was the second day.

God said: *Let the waters come together and the continents appear*.
And it was so. God called the continents "earth" and the waters "seas."
And God said: *Let the earth produce grass, plants and fruit trees*.
It was so, and God saw that it was good.
It was the third day.

Then God created the Sun, the moon and the stars.
It was the fourth day.

God said: *Let the seas produce living beings in great number and let birds fly in the heaven.*

God created the sea animals and the birds.

It was the fifth day.

God said: *Let the earth produce animals of all kinds.*

It was so and God saw that it was good.

Then God said: *Let human beings be created in my image and likeness.*

And God created man and woman in His image.

God saw all that He had done and that it was very good.

It was the sixth day.

The heaven and the Earth were populated with living beings.

The seventh day, God had completed the work He had created and He rested.

Adapted from *La Bible illustrée pour garçons et filles,* Éditions Deux coqs d'or, © 1968.

■ **How do Christians, Jews and Muslims see the Earth?**
**What did you learn about the story of Creation?**

In the story of Creation in the Christian, Jewish and Muslim traditions, it is said that on the seventh day God had completed His work.

What day of the week do Christians associate with the seventh day? Which day do Jews associate with it? Which day do Muslims associate with it? Name them.

Comparison
p. 99

# Children of the Earth

Amerindians have immense respect for our beautiful planet. As most consider it to be the mother of all life, they call it *Our Mother the Earth*. For them, all elements of nature are equal, like brothers and sisters of the same family: humans, animals, plants, air, water, fire, etc.

Amerindians represent their way of seeing the world by a symbol: the sacred circle. They consider the circle to be the shape that most closely corresponds to nature. Indeed, the Earth, the moon and the Sun are all round. The moon travels around the Earth in a circle. The seasons form a great circle, always following one another in the same order. Human life is a circle from childhood to childhood: we are born, we grow up, we become adults, and then we have our own children.

## Threddie's Info

**What do the four cardinal points in the sacred circle represent?**
In the sacred circle, the four cardinal points symbolise the great strengths all Amerindians must try to develop during their lifetimes. The North represents wisdom and courage: the South, trust; the West, self-knowledge; and the East, reflection.

According to certain Amerindian peoples, a female spirit was responsible for the creation of our world. Below is the story they have told for generations, describing how the world was created.

## The Legend of Aataentsic

Long, long ago, the world was a vast body of water, and people lived in the sky. One day, a young woman fell through a hole in the clouds. Her name was Aataentsic, which means "the one having all wisdom." Wild geese came to her rescue, supporting her with their wings.

The chief of the animals, Great Turtle, suggested the geese put her down on Great Turtle's back. Then Great Turtle asked the aquatic animals to go look for earth at the bottom of the water. One after the other, the otter, the muskrat and the beaver dove, but none of them managed to complete the mission they had been given. It was the female toad who succeeded: at the bottom of the water, she found earth clinging to the roots of the tree that had fallen at the same time as Aataentsic.

A small turtle covered the shell of the Great Turtle with the mud, making a continent. Aataentsic planted corn, beans, squash and tobacco seeds that she had brought with her from the heavenly world. This is how Aataentsic, the grandmother of us all, began to prepare for the coming of all the human beings who were to inhabit the Earth.

■ How do Amerindians see the Earth?
What did you learn about the legend of Aataentsic?

The two texts you have read present different versions of the Earth's origin.

How are they different? Compare them, and find one similarity and one difference between the two.

Comparison
p. 99

The planet Earth has abundant resources that human beings use to satisfy their needs. We often waste these resources, which results in pollution. However, protecting the planet for future generations is important to many people from various religions: Christians, Jews, Amerindians, etc. They see the Earth as a divine creation that deserves to be protected.

Find a photograph in a magazine or newspaper, or on a website, of an element of nature occurring in stories about the origin of the world: water, air, earth, fire, animal, plant, etc.

– Draw a connection between the Creation story and your photo, explaining how this element is represented in the origin of the world among Christians, Jews and Muslims.

– Draw a connection between the symbol of the sacred circle or the story of Aataentsic and your photo, explaining how this element is represented in the origin of the world among Amerindians who follow their ancestral beliefs.

## A Matter of Opinion!

p. 102

66 I saw three students in the schoolyard throw garbage on the ground. All children are polluters. 99    Mr. Beaupré

• In his statement, Mr. Beaupré makes a hasty generalization and draws an invalid conclusion.

Why is his conclusion invalid?

# Improving Relationships

Living with others can sometimes be demanding. In this module, you will learn about behaviours, attitudes and actions that can detract from group life. You will think about possible ways you can react in conflict situations.

# Regrettable Acts

Today is the day of the big departure. After weeks of preparation, the Grade Three students are leaving to spend a few days on a farm. The students are excited on the bus taking them there. For an hour, Zakary and his friends amuse themselves by waving at truckers, who respond by honking their horns.

When the bus takes a sharp turn, Zakary winds up on top of his friend Thomas. Thomas reacts by jabbing Zakary in the shoulder with his elbow. Although it hurts a bit, Zakary does not say anything, because he thinks Thomas did it as a joke.

The red roof of the barn comes into sight in the distance. Their teacher Geneviève announces that they have arrived at last. The noise level in the bus goes up, and the students are excited because they are looking forward to visiting the farm.

"Get out of the way! I want to be the first one out of the bus!" shouts Thomas, pushing Émilie and Julianne aside.

In his haste, Thomas pushes Émilie who falls over backwards. He notices that Julianne has dropped her diary on the ground in the jostling. He decides to trample on it because he thinks she looks funny wearing her new glasses.

Zakary is furious. This is not the first time he has seen Thomas behave like a bully. If Zakary did not control himself, he would yell at Thomas. But he knows that is not a good solution. Instead, as Geneviève taught them, he takes a deep breath and counts to five while thinking about what he is going to say.

"Thomas, I feel like sometimes you lack respect for the people around you. You hurt me earlier when you jabbed me with your elbow in the bus. That was not nice of you."

"Yes, but ...," says Thomas.

"Let me finish what I have to say to you, Thomas. When you were rushing to get out of the bus first, you made Émilie fall and you got Julianne's diary all dirty. Why are you always mean to Julianne? She has never done anything to you."

Thomas does not like being caught doing something wrong or being confronted. Because the other students were often scared to confront him, Thomas is astonished at Zakary speaking to him this way. Thomas, though, listened and realized that Zakary's message was clear and respectful. He even understood what Zakary may have felt when he jabbed him with his elbow. He admits to Zakary:

"I am sorry I hit you. I often have difficulty controlling myself. I am going to apologize to Émilie and Julianne. I will find a way to fix the diary I trampled on."

Zakary shakes Thomas' hand to show him that he is satisfied with their discussion of the matter. Geneviève congratulates them, because she feels they behaved very respectfully. She will mention it in the next class meeting. Their stay is getting off to a good start.

■ **Thomas behaved like a bully. What do you consider to be bullying behaviour?**

Sometimes people put down, ridicule or ignore other people because they are different. Yet we are all different.

Would it be better if we were all the same? Why?

Comparison
p. 99

**Module 6**

# Dealing With Conflict

Living with others means meeting people who think and behave differently from us. These differences can sometimes lead to situations of conflict and cause people to feel angry or frustrated. To live in harmony, we must talk to one another and resolve our conflicts. This is the story of Édouard and Audrey who were unable to resolve their disagreement.

Édouard was having so much fun playing that he threw the ball harder than he meant to. The ball hit Audrey on the arm, and she began to cry.

Édouard said to her: "You are a girl and girls are crybabies!" Audrey became even angrier and replied: "You hurt me on purpose. I do not want to play with you any more!"

Édouard answered crossly: "I do not care. In any case, I do not like playing with girls. They are all babies!" Édouard and Audrey have been in conflict ever since the incident.

A conflict may be as little as an argument or as big as a war. A conflict can happen when certain rules that help ensure friendly relationships are not respected, such as being polite, listening to and understanding others. Unresolved conflicts can get worse. So it is important to know how to deal with conflict situations.

## Different Ways of Responding

There are several ways to let people know we disagree with them. For example, we can leave, get angry, express our feelings, take a time-out or negotiate. We say that two people are negotiating when they work together to try to find a compromise they can agree on. When we are angry, it is good to stop and think things over to avoid doing something we may regret.

66 I leave without doing anything, even when I am treated unfairly. 99     Stephanie

66 When I am angry, I feel like yelling, saying something mean, hitting or crying. 99     Éric

66 I try to say how I feel respectfully and without hurting the other person. 99  Marie

66 To help myself calm down, I take a deep breath, count to five, and ask myself what I can do or say. I try to find solutions that do not hurt anyone. 99  Julie

66 The other day, I had an argument with my sister. We negotiated to resolve our dispute. We took turns saying what we wanted and we explained why we wanted it. We described how we felt. Finally, we found a solution together and were on good terms again. 99  Nicolas

■ **What could Édouard and Audrey have done to resolve their conflict in the schoolyard?**

Sometimes we have conflicts with others. We may feel angry and frustrated.

How do you resolve the conflicts you have in the classroom? in the schoolyard?

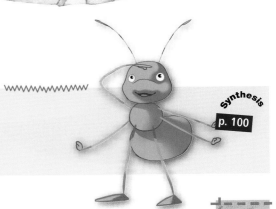

Synthesis
p. 100

**Improving Relationships**

# Standing Up to Bullying

Do you know the Wicked Witch in *The Wizard of Oz,* a story written by Lyman Frank Baum in 1900? It recounts the adventures of Dorothy, who must go to the Emerald City to ask the Wizard of Oz to send her home. The Wicked Witch tries to stop her from getting to her destination by scaring her and even tries to hurt her. In spite of everything, Dorothy manages to get back home.

In the story, Dorothy is the victim of the witch's bullying. Of course, the witch is a fictional character, but some people bully others in real life too. This type of behaviour does not promote harmony or friendly relations.

## How Can You Recognize Bullying?

Bullying can take many forms. Bullying means pushing, hitting, insulting, threatening, spreading rumours or revealing personal information about someone else, or destroying things belonging to them. It involves pressuring, threatening, or insulting people in a way that hurts and upsets them, and this behaviour is repeated frequently.

Bullies do not wear labels. They may be girls or boys. They may have good grades or bad grades, have lots of friends or none. They all have one thing in common: they are frequently mean to people who dare not defend themselves or stand up for themselves, or people who are alone. People who bully others like having power or control over others.

## How Should You Deal With Bullying?

What should you do if you are the victim of bullying? You have three choices: stand up for yourself and resist the bullying, do nothing and put up with it, or go away and ask for help.

66 When big kids make fun of me in the schoolyard, I keep calm and hold my head up high. I ask them to stop because I do not like it when other people make fun of me.99     Maël

66 My cousin's friends wanted me to take candies from the corner store without paying. I did not think it was a good idea, but I did not want to get into a disagreement with them, so I decided to leave. It took a lot of courage.99     Malory

> ❝The other day, Martin and his friends threatened me again because they wanted my lunchbox. I was fed up. I told my teacher about it and asked for help.❞  Macha

No one way of dealing with bullying is better than another. What is important is making the behaviour stop and talking about it.

■ **Bullying is a problem which can be solved. Have you ever been the victim of or witnessed such behaviour? What solutions were found?**

There are many types of conflicts.

What are the differences between an argument and bullying?

Comparison p. 99

# Reconsidering Our Behaviour

Sometimes, small acts we consider harmless can lead to conflict. Teasing a student whose coat is too small, borrowing a pencil from a classmate without asking permission, or destroying the snow fort someone else built are some such examples. When we think about what we did afterwards, we wish we could go back in time and adopt more appropriate behaviour.

## In a Few Words

When conflict arises, it is a good idea to determine the cause and find a means of resolving it.

It is also important to recognize bullying and to know how to respond appropriately.

## Your Turn

Imagine you have the power to change certain behaviours to avoid a conflict situation. With your classmates, prepare a two-part skit on conflict or bullying. Present the skit.

– In one case, a character's behaviour leads to a conflict.

– In the other, the same character's behaviour is completely different and the conflict is avoided.

## A Matter of Opinion!

p. 101

66 Teasing and bullying are two different behaviours. Teasing is poking fun at someone by making inoffensive remarks while bullying involves making someone afraid. Bullying must not be tolerated in our school! 99   The Principal

• By forbidding bullying, the principal makes a judgment of prescription.

What are the principal's reasons for forbidding bullying?

Do you think the ban is likely to be respected?

# Never to forget

Anne Frank

The Calvary cross in Saint-Joseph-de-la-Pointe-de-Lévy

The chapel at Sainte-Anne-de-Neuville

The names of cities destroyed during the Shoah

The statue of Our Lady of the Saguenay

The Kanesatake powwow in Oka

In this module, you will discover the origins and meanings of certain monuments and buildings in the province of Québec. You will also discover traces of bygone events and past religious customs that are still practised.

# Sombre Memories

This Sunday afternoon, Albert is looking at a science book at the municipal library. He is taking notes for his school project. He has chosen his topic, lasers. His father, who is a doctor, told him about possible uses for lasers in medicine. Albert has been fascinated by the topic ever since.

His big brother, Nathan, is surfing the Web on the computer. He helps Albert find information for his research.

"Nathan, did you know that the scientist who invented the laser had the same first name as I do? His name was Albert Einstein."

"Ah! Interesting," answers Nathan. "Coming? We are going to the circulation desk."

"Okay. I am taking out two comic books and two books on lasers," says Albert.

What books have you chosen?

"I chose a book on a true story," says Nathan. "It was written long ago by a girl my age. It is her diary. It is called *The Diary of Anne Frank*."

"What exactly is it about?"

**Shoah**
The attempt to exterminate European Jews by Nazi Germany during the Second World War.

**Nazi**
A person belonging to a racist political party that first appeared in Germany in 1919 and that sought to exterminate the Jewish people.

"Anne Frank lived in Europe around 1940. She and her family underwent a very difficult ordeal during the Second World War because they were Jewish. It was called the 'Shoah,' which means 'catastrophe' in Hebrew."

"During the war, European Jews were arrested by **Nazi** soldiers and imprisoned in concentration camps. Most of the imprisoned Jews died of hunger or abuse, or were killed. Several countries, including Canada, joined forces to go to war against the Nazis. Unfortunately, millions of Jews had already been exterminated."

*Anne Frank*

Albert is very upset. He thinks it is unfair and revolting for people to be victims of violence because of their religion. He asks his brother questions to help him understand.

"I do not know all the answers to your questions! Come on, we will go talk to Dad and Mom about it," says Nathan.

The two boys go to find their parents, who are reading newspapers in another part of the library. Their mother suggests they visit the **Holocaust** museum, where visitors can learn more about what happened during the Second World War.

*The names of 5000 cities containing Jewish communities that existed before the war and were destroyed during the Shoah*

Albert's father explains that in 2005 the government of Québec paid tribute to the Canadian soldiers who died in the Second World War (1939–1945). On the sixtieth anniversary of the end of the war, a section of Highway 20 was named "Autoroute du Souvenir" (or Remembrance Highway) to celebrate the courage of these soldiers.

> **Holocaust**
> The attempt
> by the Nazis to
> exterminate Jews.

■ **The Second World War left traces. What traces can you find in the text (documents, monuments, buildings, etc.)?**

*The Tomb of the Unknown Soldier, in Ottawa*

In the Second World War and the other conflicts in which Canada has taken part, 27 000 Canadian soldiers died whose bodies were never found or identified. In spring 2000, the Canadian government erected a monument to pay homage to them: The Tomb of the Unknown Soldier, in Ottawa.

A date has been set aside in the calendar for remembering these soldiers: November 11th.

What is this day called? Find out its name.

Description p. 99

# Heritage Monuments

Different elements of our environment reveal parts of our religious past. There are numerous Catholic monuments in Québec because Catholicism has been the most widespread religion here for centuries. These monuments are part of the heritage our society passes on to future generations.

## Wayside Crosses

In the 17th century, many French Catholic immigrants settled in New France. Most of the newly arrived colonists were farmers. As the colonists settled on their land, roads were built. A large cross was erected every time a new road was opened. The colonists worked long days in the fields, right up

*The Calvary cross at Saint-Joseph-de-la-Pointe-de-Lévy*

until sunset. So they would go to the wayside crosses to pray rather than going all the way to church.

There are still approximately 3000 wayside crosses in Québec at the entrance to cities and villages. Of these, 25 are considered provincial treasures because they are exceptional works of art and were erected by 1920 at the latest.

*A wayside cross erected at the side of Chemin Principal in Notre-Dame-des-Sept-Douleurs*

## Threddie's Info

**How do we protect historical monuments in Québec?**

In Québec, there is an organization responsible for looking after the conservation of historical monuments. One of the roles of the *Commission des biens culturels du Québec* is to ensure that a monument's original appearance is preserved when it is restored.

# Statues

Catholics also had statues built in Québec. Their places of worship, churches, are decorated with them. These statues can also be found outdoors, in village centres and the countryside.

## Our Lady of the Saguenay

In the winter of 1878, a travelling salesman had to cross the Saguenay River. The ice broke under his weight and he fell into the water. Unable to pull himself out, he prayed to Mary, the mother of Jesus, to save him. Then, he managed to reach solid ground. He considered it a miracle. To thank Mary, he had a statue built in her honour.

*The Our Lady of the Saguenay statue by Louis Jobin (1845–1928) on Cape Trinité*

## Saint George Slaying the Dragon

In 1912, the parish of Saint-Georges-Ouest, in the Beauce region, erected a monument in honour of its **patron saint**, Saint George, a Christian prince who was **martyred** and died in the year 303. Legend has it that he freed a town by fighting a dragon.

*Louis Jobin's statue of Saint George slaying the dragon has been moved inside the church. A reproduction is on display outdoors*

**Patron saint**
The saint to whom a church is dedicated.

**To martyr**
To torture or make suffer.

■ Is there a monument (statue, sculpture) near where you live? What does it represent?

Many monuments in Québec serve to remind us of important events or historic figures. Others are simply expressions of an artist's world-view.

What is the use of such monuments? Explain your point of view.

*Les Clochards Célestes, statue created by Pierreyves Angers in 1983*

Explanation

p. 100

# Living Traditions

Our environment contains many traces of our religious past. Such traces may be preserved in stone or wood as monuments or statues, but they may also be living traces. Sometimes large numbers of people who share the same religion gather together in the streets to commemorate an event, or to celebrate or pray.

## Stations of the Cross

During Holy Week, many Catholics attend religious celebrations at church. Some also do the Stations of the Cross together to commemorate the final moments of the life of Jesus. Using texts from the New Testament, the priest tells the story of The Passion: how Jesus was made to walk, carrying his cross, to the place where he was hung on it and died.

In the past, the vast majority of Québec Catholics did the Stations of the Cross. Although the tradition is less widespread nowadays, it is still practised here. In Jerusalem, the city where Jesus died nearly 2000 years ago, thousands of **pilgrims** still gather every year at Easter time to do the Stations of the Cross.

**Pilgrim**
A person who travels to a holy place to pray.

*Christians doing the Stations of the Cross in Jerusalem*

# Torch Processions

Torch processions were another very popular practice in Québec in days gone by. The people of the parish would gather in the evening, candle lanterns in hand, and walk through the streets of their city or village to honour a saint. All along the way, they would pray, asking the famous saint for favours. The atmosphere of the procession was calm and contemplative. As it was a long walk, the procession would stop at different points. Thus, many villages built a chapel less than one kilometre from the church. That way, people could enter to rest a little there before continuing the procession.

Although this type of torch procession is less frequent nowadays, many Catholics are committed to preserving the tradition. Some parishes organize torch processions on Saturday evenings in the summer. Even today, one of the most popular is a procession dedicated to Saint Anne, considered by Catholics and Orthodox Christians to be the grandmother of Jesus. Many of the people who take part in it ask the Saint to heal loved ones who are gravely ill or friends in difficulty.

■ **What have you learned about these two Catholic traditions: the Stations of the Cross and torch processions?**

Once strictly a religious event, torch processions are now also held by non-religious groups. People come together and march to commemorate tragic events, to raise funds for good causes, to celebrate important events, etc.

People come together for other events, causes and celebrations. Which ones? Name them.

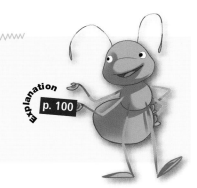

Explanation
p. 100

# Gatherings Like Those of the Past

In Québec, some gatherings are customs that have existed for centuries. Native peoples, the first inhabitants of our land, continue to come together in the same way their ancestors did. Such gatherings are opportunities for them to celebrate and pray.

Powwows are an ancient tradition among many Amerindian peoples. Before going to a powwow, some Amerindians purify their cloths and drums with sacred herbs to scare away bad spirits. Powwows usually begin with a procession of the elders of the community dressed in their traditional costumes. The drummers accompany the procession with their music. Powwows provide an opportunity to eat traditional foods like **bannock** or moose. As is customary, many people exchange presents. Even non-Natives participate, for example, by coming to listen to the songs and oral tales that the Amerindians pass on from one generation to the next.

**Bannock**
A flatbread that is a staple food of Amerindians.

Many Amerindian peoples organize weekend-long powwows in the summer. Some of these gatherings attract over 1000 people.

*A platter of bannock*

*The Kanesatake powwow in Oka*

## In a Few Words

Numerous monuments or buildings throughout Québec have historical value as they remind us of the history of the people of this province. For example, the Jewish community has set up a museum that commemorates the Holocaust. Among other things, Catholics have erected wayside crosses, statues and churches. Protestants and Orthodox have also built buildings such as churches and schools. Some religious traditions still alive today also bear witness to our past, such as torch processions, the Stations of the Cross, and powwows.

## Your Turn

Choose a tradition, monument or building that is related to a religious tradition. Do research to describe the religious tradition to which this form of religious expression is related, its meaning and the reason for its existence.

Present your research and your discoveries to your classmates.

## A Matter of Opinion!

p. 101

66 I prefer to live in a country that is at peace rather than a country at war. 99 Carlos

• In his statement, Carlos makes a judgment of preference.

What questions might you ask Carlos to find out the reasons for his preference?

# Religious Treasures

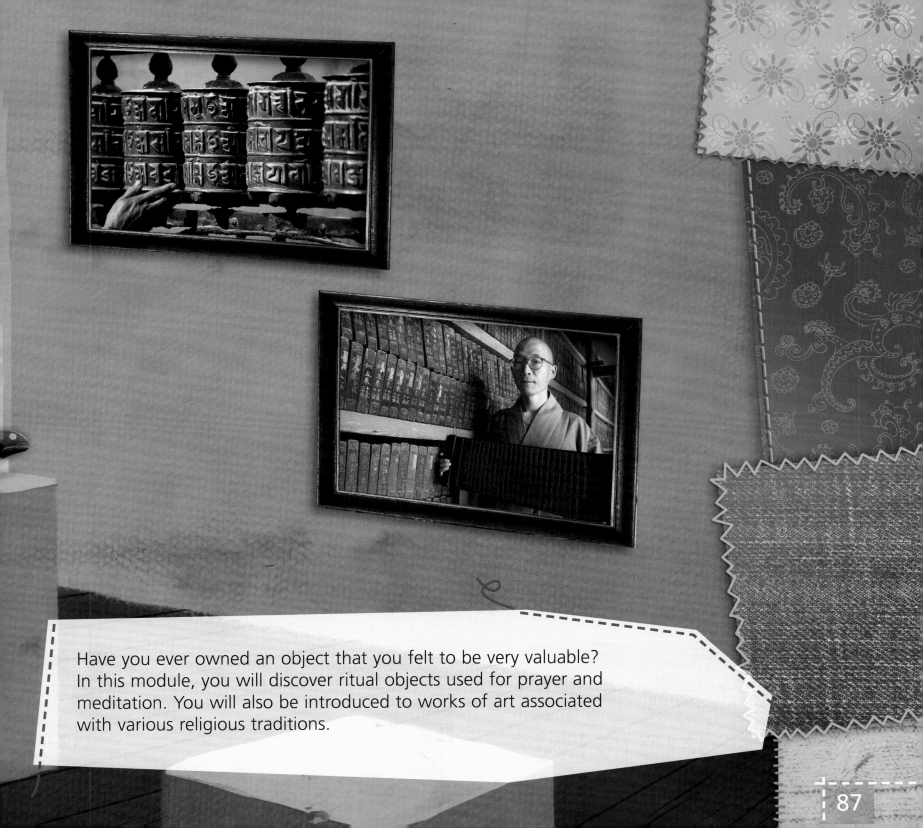

Have you ever owned an object that you felt to be very valuable? In this module, you will discover ritual objects used for prayer and meditation. You will also be introduced to works of art associated with various religious traditions.

# A Visit to the Museum

One Sunday in the spring, Camille and Cédric are waiting impatiently for their grandmother Laura. She has offered to take them to explore the museums. They are going to regularly visit new museums and exhibits together.

"Hello, my loves! Are you ready? Today, we are going to discover Rodin," announces their grandmother.

"But I thought we were going to the museum," says Cédric.

"We are going to the museum. That is where you are going to learn about this great French artist," answers Grandmother Laura.

"What are we going to see?" asks Camille.

"You are going to see works of art: sculptures, paintings, and beautiful objects that must be carefully protected. Such objects are often grouped together in collections in museums," explains their grandmother.

"But where do the works of art in museums come from?" asks Cédric.

"They come from all over. Sometimes they are lent by other museums or their owners who want as many people as possible to see them," answers the grandmother as she drives.

A U G U S T E
RODIN
THE MAN AND HIS WORK

When they arrive at the museum, Grandmother Laura turns off her phone and asks Cédric to throw his apple into the garbage can near the entrance. Then she leads her grandchildren into the first room of the exhibit.

"Here is a bronze sculpture called *The Thinker*. It is a reproduction of a work Rodin created over 100 years ago."

"What is the sculpture of?" asks Camille.

"It is of a man who is deep in thought and seems to have a choice to make," replies the grandmother.

"I like the slightly shiny colour, adds Cédric," going up to touch the sculpture.

Grandmother Laura reminds her grandson of one of the museum rules.

"Cédric, I know you do not want to damage the sculpture. It is best not to touch works of art in museums. That way, they can be better **preserved**," explains his grandmother.

Cédric stops and pulls his hand back, because he understands the reason for the rule and agrees with it.

> To preserve
> To protect, to keep from dammage.

"I think Rodin had a lot of talent. I am happy to be discovering him with you, Grandma," says Cédric.

■ **What rules must we respect when we visit museums?**

Cédric, Camille and their grandmother followed the museum rules during their visit.

Why are there rules in museums?

Do you think it is important to respect them? Why?

Explanation
p. 100

# Ritual Objects

For Catholics and the Orthodox, saints are people who have led exemplary religious lives.

All religions have ritual objects, which are objects and symbols related to religious practices like prayer or meditation. Such objects are considered by believers to be sacred or worthy of respect.

A rosary

The Christian Gallery

The Nativity

Bible

A cross

A Bible

A prayer book

In their prayers, Christians speak to God the Father or to His Son, Jesus, to thank them or ask for forgiveness or advice. They may read a prayer, recite one they have learned by heart, or use words and gestures of their own. The Bible and the **missal** contain the *Lord's Prayer*. It is a Christian prayer Jesus taught his disciples to teach them to pray. Some Christians, such as Catholics and the Orthodox, use **rosaries** to pray.

The Native Peoples Gallery

An Amerindian dance

A drum

A prayer rattle

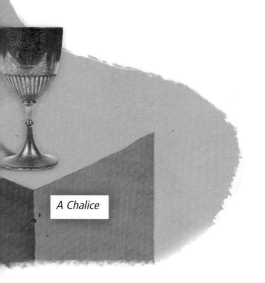

A Chalice

Some Native peoples who follow their ancestral beliefs believe that the elements of nature are inhabited by spirits. Song and dance are ways for them to communicate with these spirits and to thank the Earth for all its resources. They like to express their joy through music and dance.

In some communities, the spiritual guide, the shaman, uses musical instruments decorated with **pictograms** to heal the sick. Prayer rattles are used to call forth the spirit of life. They sing in a circle around the drum, a ritual object that represents the Earth. The beating of the drum helps the shaman communicate with the spirit world.

**Missal**
A book containing the hymns, prayers, readings and actions in Catholic and Orthodox religious celebrations.

**Rosary**
A necklace of beads, each of them corresponding to a separate prayer, which one slides through one's fingers as one prays.

**Pictogram**
A small symbolic drawing used by Native peoples as a form of writing.

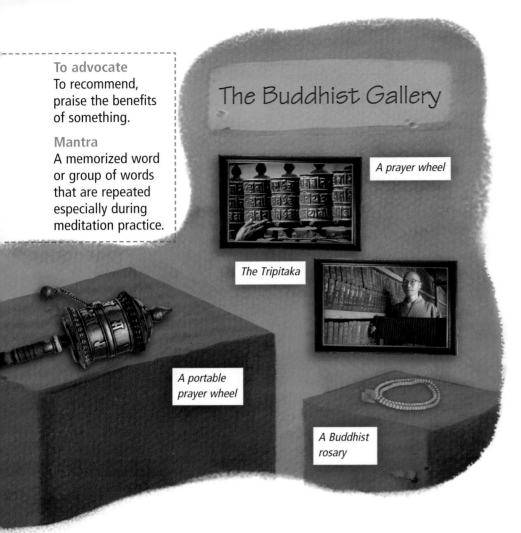
**To advocate**
To recommend, praise the benefits of something.

**Mantra**
A memorized word or group of words that are repeated especially during meditation practice.

A prayer wheel

The Tripitaka

A portable prayer wheel

A Buddhist rosary

Buddhists consult the *Tripitaka,* a series of texts that presents the rules to be followed to respect the teachings of Buddha, **advocating** a life without violence.

Buddhists practise meditation. To do it, they recite a **mantra** while listening to the sound of their voices rising and falling. This exercise is a form of prayer that helps them concentrate better. The rosary helps them count the number of times they have repeated the mantra. Some Buddhists use a prayer wheel. This is an object that contains a roll of paper on which the sacred mantra has been written several times. When it is turned, the wheel makes the mantra turn and the mantra repeats itself.

■ **With which religious traditions do you associate the ritual objects shown?**

A Tibetan mandala

Some Buddhists contemplate mandalas. The practice consists of gazing at these images until you feel as if you are a part of them. It helps Buddhists clear their minds of thoughts of everyday life. The mandala has become a widespread art form. It is a circle containing a geometric, symbolic image of the universe for Hindus and Buddhists. Mandalas are used as an aid to meditation.

Have you ever seen mandalas? Where? If not, where could you see some?

p. 99

Description

# A Colourful Exhibit

There are different types of museums, such as art museums, science museums, and history museums. In all of them, you can see objects related to various topics.

## In a Few Words

Ritual objects are often used in prayer and meditation. These objects vary from one religious tradition to another, and are considered sacred because they are associated with religious practices. Religion has even inspired great works by many artists.

## Your Turn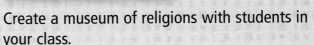

Create a museum of religions with students in your class.

– In a team, choose a form of religious expression you have seen during the year and think of an original way of presenting it. It may be a religious figure, object, symbol, event, place, street name, story, etc.

– Write a text that presents and describes the form of religious expression you have chosen, specifying with which religious tradition it is associated.

With students in your class, establish the rules to be respected in your museum.

## A Matter of Opinion!

p. 102

❝ Alexandre does not dress the same way we do, so we are not going to choose him to be a part of our team for the museum of religions project.❞     Suzie

• Suzie is making a personal attack in her statement.

  Why is it a personal attack?

# The Dialogue Box

Hi! My name is Unik. I live in a colony with other ants of the same kind. We are like the pieces of fabric in a quilt, similar, but also very different from one another.

When I have difficult choices to make, I try to find a solution that will foster harmony while respecting each individual in the colony. To do that, I apply some rules that encourage dialogue.

Dialogue is essential in a colony. You could compare it to the thread joining the pieces of fabric in a quilt. Dialogue helps me get to know myself better and to better understand and respect others.

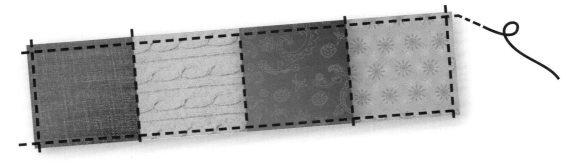

The following pages will provide you with some helpful hints. Use them to answer the questions on Ethics (green patch) or Religious Culture (yellow patch), or in the  feature.

# Forms of Dialogue

A dialogue can take different forms.

**1** A **conversation** is an exchange between two or more people. During a conversation, people share their ideas or experiences.

Érika and Maélie are having a serious conversation, telling each other about their summer holidays.

**2** A **discussion** can take place between two or more people. It is an organized exchange of opinions or ideas. During a discussion, people listen carefully to the opinions and ideas expressed, and try to understand them properly.

Marco, Sabrina and Antoine are having a serious discussion. They take turns saying what they think of a film they just saw. They discuss what was best about the film and what they thought did not work as well.

**3** A **narration** is an oral or written account of a series of facts or events.

Raphaëlle tells Sylvianne how she broke her arm in gym class.

**4** A **deliberation** is when a group of people try to reach a common decision about something. First, everyone thinks about the situation together. Then they try to determine what is important and what must be considered. Finally, they evaluate the possible consequences of the different suggestions, and then they make a decision.

Sarah, Louisa, Mathias and Édouard are planning a sports activity for the class. They thought it over and noted that they all have different preferences. They remember that Joël has a broken leg. They discuss the matter and agree to choose an activity in which the entire class can participate. They decide to play hockey. They suggest to Joël that he be the goalie, sitting in his wheelchair.

**5** An **interview** takes place between two or more people. The interviewer asks about the other person's activities, ideas, experiences, etc.

Jérémie asks Jade about her best holiday memories. She tells him about her experience camping, and the fishing trip she went on in a canoe. Jérémie questions Jade to learn more details.

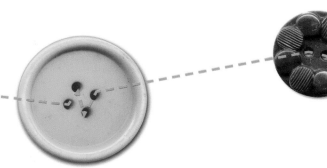

# Rules for Effective Dialogue

Certain rules promote effective and respectful dialogue.
Below are a few.

## Before ...

 **1** Think of what you can say and what you already know about the topic. Think about your preferences, feelings, ideas and opinions.

 **2** Decide which things are important and how you are going to present them.

## During ...

 **3** Wait for your turn to speak.

 **4** Express yourself clearly and calmly. Pay attention to your gestures, changes in your voice, and your facial expression.

 **5** Make sure you express yourself in a way that encourages harmony, friendly relationships and mutual respect.

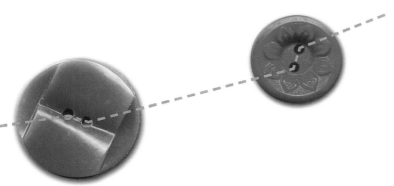

**6** Use examples or explanations to support the points you raise.

 **7** Listen carefully when someone else is speaking. Respect that person's ideas and opinions. Pay attention to the speaker's gestures, changes in voice, and facial expressions.

 **8** Ask questions to help you understand other people's ideas.

## Afterwards …

 **9** Compare the different ideas. Note what caused tension or conflict, if any. Notice any agreement among several people.

 **10** Go back over the dialogue.

– Did your ideas change? Why?

– What did you learn about the topic and about how to have a dialogue?

– Did the dialogue help you understand other people's ideas better?

**The Dialogue Box**

# Ways for Developing a Point of View

In a dialogue you can develop your point of view and present your ideas in different ways. Below are a few. Your choice of words is important.

**1** Providing a **description** of something means giving as much information about it as possible. To decide what information you should give, ask yourself the following questions: Who? What? Where? When? How? Why? How much? How many?

*Example:* Thomas describes a community service organization.

"The Society of Saint Vincent de Paul has existed for many years. Its role is to help people living in poverty. Its members collect clothing, furniture and toys. All these goods are given to people in need. The organization has helped thousands of people since it was first founded."

**2** To make a **comparison** is to find the differences and similarities between situations, people or things.

*Example:* Judith compares the rules of conduct in her school with those in another school.

"When the bell rings at the end of recess at my school, everyone goes inside right away. We have to enter calmly and talk softly. Things are a bit different at my cousin's school. When the bell rings there, students silently line up in front of the door. They must wait for the signal before they may go in. They have to enter calmly too, but they are not allowed to whisper. There must be total silence."

**3** To provide a **synthesis** is to summarize the important elements of a situation or a fact.

*Example:* Marilou provides a synthesis of the story of Creation according to the Jewish and Christian faiths.

"The story of Creation says that on the first day, God created the day and the night. On the second day, God created the sky. On the third day, God created the sea, the continents and the plants. On the fourth day, God created the Sun, the moon and the stars. On the fifth day, God created the animals of the sea and the birds. On the sixth day, God created the animals of the land as well as man and woman. Finally, on the seventh day, God had finished his work and he rested."

**4** To give an **explanation** is to introduce people to something or help them understand its meaning. To do that, you use examples, give details and define new or difficult words.

*Example:* The school principal explains one of the school's safety regulations.

"Throwing snowballs in the playground is dangerous and will no longer be permitted. The ice in snowballs can injure the people who are hit by them. This rule will be in effect in the morning, before classes start, during morning recess, at lunchtime, during afternoon recess, and during the after-school childcare program."

# Ways of Examining a Point of View

Knowing how to examine a point of view is useful for effective dialogue. It helps you tell the difference between the various types of judgments you can make, and to recognize the types of statements that may make dialogue more difficult.

## Different Types of Judgment

Three types of judgment are given below. You can ask certain questions to help you recognize them and better understand other people's ideas and opinions.

 A **judgment of preference** expresses a taste or preference.

 I like Halloween celebrations.

 I am sure you have a reason. Why do you like them?

 A **judgment of prescription** is a statement in which you make a recommendation, give an order or set a rule.

We must respect the environment.

Why is that important? Do you think it is possible to respect that rule?

 A **judgment of reality** is a statement in which you tell about an event or give a piece of information. The judgment may be false!

 Young people are concerned about their health.

 Where does this information come from? From an observation you made? From someone who told it to you? From someone who knows a lot about the topic? Can you check this information in a book or by asking a resource person?

# Statements That Make Dialogue More Difficult

Some types of statements can make dialogue more difficult. Avoid using them. Practise recognizing them when other people use them.

 **1** ## Hasty Generalizations

I bought a pair of shoes because I liked the way they looked. They are uncomfortable! I will never buy shoes that look good because shoes that look good hurt your feet.

Threddie, a single observation is not enough for you to form an opinion!

 **2** ## Personal Attacks

Marc-Olivier is often sick. What would he know about how to get in shape?

Threddie, when *you judge Marc-Olivier like that you* are making a personal attack. Let him speak for himself instead. You might discover he does know how to get in shape.

 **3** ## Appeal to the Crowd

My friends did not like downhill skiing. So I have decided I am never going to do it, because it is a really boring sport.

Threddie, that is just the opinion of a small group of people. Your opinion may be different from that of people you like, or it may be the same. You may also have the same opinion as people you do not like.

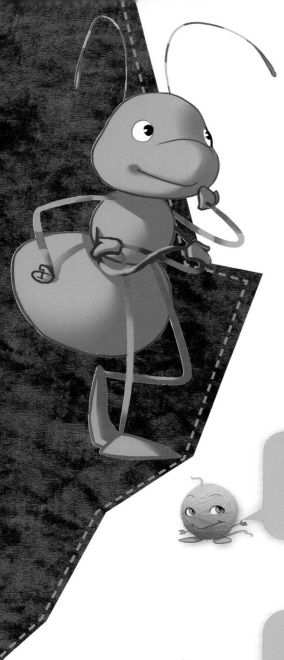

# Glossary

| | |
|---|---|
| **Bannock** | A flatbread that is a staple food of Amerindians. |
| **Consensus** | A common decision, agreement reached in a group. |
| **Divine Liturgy** | A celebration for which the Orthodox come together on Sunday. |
| **Empathy** | Ability to put oneself in the place of another, to understand what the other person feels. |
| **Hebrew** | That which relates to the Hebrews, the ancestors of the Jewish people. |
| **Holocaust** | The attempt by the Nazis to exterminate Jews. |
| **Lotus position** | Meditation position with the right foot on the left thigh, the left foot on the right thigh and the body as straight as possible. |
| **Mantra** | A memorized word or group of words that are repeated especially during meditation practice. |
| **Mass** | A catholic celebration representing Jesus' last meal. |
| **Missal** | A book containing the hymns, prayers, readings and actions in Catholic and Orthodox religious celebrations. |
| **Muezzin** | The person responsible for calling the Muslim faithful to prayer. |
| **Nazi** | A person belonging to a racist political party that first appeared in Germany in 1919 and that sought to exterminate the Jewish people. |
| **Patron saint** | The saint to whom a church is dedicated. |
| **Pictogram** | A small symbolic drawing used by Native peoples as a form of writing. |
| **Pilgrim** | A person who travels to a holy place to pray. |
| **Place of worship** | A place where believers gather together to pay homage to a deity. |
| **Preaching** | A speech to an assembly of believers |
| **Reciprocally** | In the same way to each other |
| **Rosary** | A necklace of beads, each of them corresponding to a separate prayer, which one slides through one's fingers as one prays. |
| **Sermon** | A speech by a pastor or lay preacher and based on one or more biblical texts. |
| **Service** | A gathering in which Protestants come together, generally held on Sunday. |
| **Shoah** | The attempt to exterminate European Jews by Nazi Germany during the Second World War. |
| **Tefillin** | A pair of boxes containing excerpts from the Torah, which certain practising Jewish men wear on the forehead and left arm during prayer. |
| **To advocate** | To recommend, praise the benefits of something. |
| **To martyr** | To torture or make suffer. |
| **To preserve** | To protect, to keep from dammage. |
| **Volunteer** | A person who helps another freely and without being paid. |